EMMANUEL JOSEPH

The Policy of Profit, Rethinking Business Through the Lens of Politics and Society

Copyright © 2025 by Emmanuel Joseph

All rights reserved. No part of this publication may be reproduced, stored or transmitted in any form or by any means, electronic, mechanical, photocopying, recording, scanning, or otherwise without written permission from the publisher. It is illegal to copy this book, post it to a website, or distribute it by any other means without permission.

First edition

This book was professionally typeset on Reedsy.
Find out more at reedsy.com

Contents

1	Chapter 1: The Intersection of Business and Politics	1
2	Chapter 2: The Role of Regulation in Shaping Business...	3
3	Chapter 3: The Impact of Corporate Lobbying on Public Policy	5
4	Chapter 4: Social Responsibility and Ethical Business...	7
5	Chapter 5: The Influence of Globalization on Business and...	9
6	Chapter 6: The Role of Technology in Business and Society	11
7	Chapter 7: The Influence of Corporate Governance on Business...	13
8	Chapter 8: The Role of Business in Addressing Climate Change	15
9	Chapter 9: The Influence of Corporate Culture on Business...	17
10	Chapter 10: The Role of Corporate Philanthropy in Society	19
11	Chapter 11: The Role of Business in Promoting Social Justice	21
12	Chapter 12: The Future of Business: Integrating Profit and...	23
13	Chapter 13: Navigating Ethical Dilemmas in Business	25
14	Chapter 14: The Role of Innovation in Driving Business...	27
15	Chapter 15: Building Resilient Businesses for the Future	29

1

Chapter 1: The Intersection of Business and Politics

Paragraph 1: The relationship between business and politics is a complex and multifaceted one. Historically, the two spheres have often been seen as separate entities, with business focusing on profit-making and politics dealing with governance and public welfare. However, in reality, the boundaries between these two realms are increasingly blurred. Governments create the regulatory frameworks within which businesses operate, and businesses, in turn, influence political processes through lobbying, campaign contributions, and other means. This chapter explores the historical evolution of this relationship and sets the stage for a deeper examination of how businesses and politics influence each other.

Paragraph 2: The rise of globalization and the increasing interconnectedness of economies have further intensified the relationship between business and politics. Multinational corporations operate across multiple jurisdictions, each with its own set of rules and regulations. This has led to a complex web of interactions between businesses and political entities at local, national, and international levels. The pursuit of profit by businesses often necessitates navigating this intricate landscape, leading to strategic alliances, partnerships, and sometimes conflicts with political bodies. Understanding these dynamics is crucial for comprehending the contemporary business environment.

Paragraph 3: Additionally, businesses are not just passive players in the political arena; they actively shape it. Through lobbying efforts, businesses attempt to influence legislation and regulation in ways that favor their interests. Campaign contributions and other forms of political engagement allow businesses to support candidates and parties that align with their goals. This bidirectional influence raises important questions about the balance of power and the implications for democratic governance. To what extent should businesses be allowed to exert influence over political processes, and what safeguards are necessary to ensure that this influence does not undermine the public good?

Paragraph 4: In recent years, there has been a growing recognition of the need for businesses to engage in social and political issues. Consumers, employees, and other stakeholders increasingly expect businesses to take stands on important societal issues, from climate change to social justice. This trend reflects a broader shift in the understanding of the role of business in society. No longer is profit the sole metric of success; businesses are increasingly judged by their social and political impact. This chapter concludes by exploring the implications of this shift for the future of business and its relationship with politics.

Would you like to proceed with more chapters, or do you have any specific topics in mind that you'd like each chapter to cover?

continue to other chapters

Great! Let's continue with the next chapters.

2

Chapter 2: The Role of Regulation in Shaping Business Practices

Paragraph 1: Regulation is a crucial mechanism through which governments influence business practices. Regulatory frameworks establish the rules and standards that businesses must adhere to, ensuring a level playing field and protecting public interests. These regulations can cover a wide range of areas, including environmental protection, labor rights, consumer safety, and financial transparency. By setting these parameters, governments can prevent harmful business practices and promote ethical behavior. This chapter delves into the various types of regulations and their impact on businesses.

Paragraph 2: One significant aspect of regulation is its ability to drive innovation and improvement within industries. Contrary to the perception that regulations stifle growth, they can actually spur businesses to develop new technologies and processes to comply with standards. For instance, environmental regulations have led to the creation of green technologies and sustainable business practices. Similarly, regulations in the financial sector have prompted the development of robust risk management and compliance systems. This chapter explores how regulations can serve as catalysts for positive change and enhance industry standards.

Paragraph 3: However, the implementation and enforcement of regulations are not without challenges. Businesses often face compliance costs and administrative burdens, which can be particularly onerous for small and medium-sized enterprises (SMEs). Additionally, there is the risk of regulatory capture, where powerful businesses influence regulators to create favorable conditions for themselves, potentially undermining the intended goals of regulation. This chapter examines these challenges and discusses the importance of designing effective and equitable regulatory frameworks that balance the needs of businesses and society.

Paragraph 4: The global nature of modern business further complicates regulatory efforts. Multinational corporations operate across multiple jurisdictions, each with its own regulatory environment. This creates a complex landscape where businesses must navigate varying rules and standards. International cooperation and harmonization of regulations can help address these challenges and ensure that businesses operate under consistent frameworks. This chapter concludes by discussing the role of international bodies and agreements in shaping global regulatory standards and fostering collaboration between countries.

3

Chapter 3: The Impact of Corporate Lobbying on Public Policy

Paragraph 1: Corporate lobbying is a powerful tool that businesses use to influence public policy. Through lobbying efforts, businesses seek to shape legislation and regulation in ways that align with their interests. This can involve direct interactions with lawmakers, funding research and advocacy groups, or participating in industry associations. Lobbying can have significant impacts on the policy-making process, often swaying decisions that affect entire industries and economies. This chapter provides an overview of corporate lobbying and its effects on public policy.

Paragraph 2: While lobbying can lead to positive outcomes by ensuring that lawmakers are informed about industry perspectives, it also raises concerns about the balance of power and transparency. The influence of well-funded corporate lobbyists can overshadow the voices of smaller businesses, grassroots organizations, and ordinary citizens. This chapter explores the ethical considerations of corporate lobbying and the potential for conflicts of interest. It also highlights the importance of transparency and accountability in lobbying activities to maintain public trust in the political process.

Paragraph 3: The impact of corporate lobbying is particularly pronounced in industries with significant economic and social implications, such as healthcare, finance, and energy. Decisions made in these sectors can have far-reaching consequences for public health, financial stability, and environmental sustainability. This chapter examines case studies where corporate lobbying has played a pivotal role in shaping policy outcomes, both positively and negatively. By analyzing these examples, readers can gain a deeper understanding of the complexities and controversies surrounding corporate lobbying.

Paragraph 4: In response to concerns about the influence of corporate lobbying, various measures have been proposed and implemented to regulate lobbying activities. These include mandatory disclosure of lobbying expenditures, limits on campaign contributions, and the establishment of lobbying registries. This chapter concludes by discussing the effectiveness of these measures and the ongoing efforts to ensure that lobbying serves the public interest. It also considers the role of civil society and advocacy groups in counterbalancing corporate influence and promoting more equitable policymaking.

4

Chapter 4: Social Responsibility and Ethical Business Practices

Paragraph 1: Social responsibility and ethical business practices have become increasingly important in today's world. Businesses are expected to go beyond profit-making and contribute positively to society. This includes addressing social, environmental, and economic issues, and ensuring that their operations do not harm communities or the planet. This chapter explores the principles of corporate social responsibility (CSR) and how businesses can integrate ethical practices into their strategies.

Paragraph 2: One key aspect of CSR is sustainability. Businesses are recognizing the need to adopt sustainable practices that minimize their environmental impact. This includes reducing carbon emissions, conserving natural resources, and promoting eco-friendly products and services. By prioritizing sustainability, businesses can contribute to the fight against climate change and protect the environment for future generations. This chapter examines the various ways in which businesses can implement sustainable practices and the benefits they can reap from doing so.

Paragraph 3: Another important dimension of social responsibility is addressing social and economic inequalities. Businesses have the power to create positive social change by promoting diversity and inclusion, supporting local communities, and ensuring fair labor practices. This chapter discusses the role of businesses in addressing social issues and the strategies they can use to promote social justice. It also highlights the importance of stakeholder engagement and the need for businesses to listen to and collaborate with their stakeholders.

Paragraph 4: Ethical business practices are not only about doing good but also about building trust and credibility. Businesses that prioritize ethics and transparency are more likely to gain the trust of their customers, employees, and investors. This chapter explores the relationship between ethical practices and business success, and how businesses can develop and maintain a strong ethical culture. It concludes by discussing the role of leadership in promoting ethics and the importance of setting a positive example at the top.

5

Chapter 5: The Influence of Globalization on Business and Society

Paragraph 1: Globalization has fundamentally changed the way businesses operate and interact with society. The integration of markets, technologies, and cultures has created new opportunities and challenges for businesses. This chapter explores the impact of globalization on business practices, market dynamics, and societal trends. It examines how businesses can navigate the complexities of a globalized world and leverage globalization to their advantage.

Paragraph 2: One of the key benefits of globalization is the ability to access new markets and expand business operations beyond national borders. This has allowed businesses to reach a larger customer base, diversify their revenue streams, and increase their competitiveness. However, globalization also brings challenges, such as increased competition, cultural differences, and the need to comply with diverse regulatory environments. This chapter discusses the strategies businesses can use to succeed in the global marketplace and the importance of cultural sensitivity and adaptability.

Paragraph 3: Globalization has also had a significant impact on labor markets and employment practices. The outsourcing of jobs to countries with lower labor costs has created economic opportunities for some, while leading to job losses and economic dislocation for others. This chapter examines the implications of globalization for workers and the ways in which businesses can ensure fair and equitable labor practices in a globalized economy. It also highlights the role of international labor standards and the need for businesses to respect workers' rights.

Paragraph 4: The social and cultural dimensions of globalization are equally important. The exchange of ideas, values, and cultural practices has led to greater cross-cultural understanding and collaboration. However, it has also raised concerns about cultural homogenization and the erosion of local traditions. This chapter explores the cultural impact of globalization and the role of businesses in promoting cultural diversity and preserving local heritage. It concludes by discussing the importance of corporate social responsibility in addressing the social and cultural challenges of globalization.

6

Chapter 6: The Role of Technology in Business and Society

Paragraph 1: Technology has revolutionized the way businesses operate and interact with society. From automation and artificial intelligence to digital communication and e-commerce, technological advancements have transformed every aspect of business. This chapter explores the impact of technology on business practices, productivity, and customer engagement. It examines how businesses can leverage technology to gain a competitive edge and drive innovation.

Paragraph 2: One significant area where technology has made a profound impact is data analytics. The ability to collect, analyze, and interpret vast amounts of data has enabled businesses to make more informed decisions, understand customer behavior, and optimize their operations. This chapter discusses the role of data analytics in business strategy and the importance of data-driven decision-making. It also highlights the ethical considerations and privacy concerns associated with data collection and usage.

Paragraph 3: Technology has also facilitated the rise of the gig economy and remote work. The proliferation of digital platforms and communication tools has enabled individuals to work flexibly and businesses to tap into a global talent pool. This chapter examines the benefits and challenges of the gig economy and remote work, including issues related to labor rights, job security, and work-life balance. It also explores how businesses can adapt to these trends and create inclusive and supportive work environments.

Paragraph 4: The rapid pace of technological change presents both opportunities and risks for businesses. While technology can drive growth and innovation, it can also disrupt traditional business models and create new challenges. This chapter concludes by discussing the importance of staying ahead of technological trends and investing in research and development. It also emphasizes the need for businesses to adopt a proactive approach to managing technological risks and ensuring that their technological advancements align with their ethical values and social responsibilities.

7

Chapter 7: The Influence of Corporate Governance on Business Performance

Paragraph 1: Corporate governance refers to the systems and processes through which businesses are directed and controlled. Effective corporate governance is essential for ensuring that businesses operate in a transparent, accountable, and ethical manner. This chapter explores the principles of corporate governance and their impact on business performance. It examines the role of boards of directors, executive leadership, and shareholders in shaping corporate governance practices.

Paragraph 2: One key aspect of corporate governance is the alignment of interests between management and shareholders. This alignment is crucial for ensuring that businesses prioritize long-term value creation over short-term gains. This chapter discusses the importance of incentive structures, performance metrics, and shareholder engagement in promoting aligned interests. It also highlights the challenges of balancing the demands of different stakeholders and the potential conflicts that can arise.

Paragraph 3: Transparency and accountability are fundamental principles of corporate governance. Businesses must provide accurate and timely information to their stakeholders and ensure that their decision-making processes are open and accountable. This chapter explores the role of financial reporting, audits, and regulatory compliance in promoting transparency and accountability. It also discusses the importance of ethical leadership and the need for businesses to foster a culture of integrity.

Paragraph 4: The effectiveness of corporate governance practices can have a significant impact on business performance. Strong governance practices can enhance a company's reputation, attract investment, and improve operational efficiency. Conversely, weak governance can lead to scandals, financial losses, and legal liabilities. This chapter concludes by discussing the relationship between corporate governance and business success and the ways in which businesses can strengthen their governance frameworks.

8

Chapter 8: The Role of Business in Addressing Climate Change

Paragraph 1: Climate change is one of the most pressing challenges facing humanity today. Businesses have a critical role to play in mitigating the impacts of climate change and transitioning to a low-carbon economy. This chapter explores the responsibilities and opportunities for businesses in addressing climate change. It examines the strategies that businesses can adopt to reduce their carbon footprint and contribute to global efforts to combat climate change.

Paragraph 2: One of the primary ways businesses can address climate change is by adopting sustainable practices. This includes reducing greenhouse gas emissions, improving energy efficiency, and investing in renewable energy sources. By integrating sustainability into their operations and supply chains, businesses can minimize their environmental impact and promote a more sustainable future. This chapter discusses the various approaches to sustainability and the benefits of adopting green practices.

Paragraph 3: In addition to operational changes, businesses can also influence climate policy through advocacy and collaboration. By supporting policies and initiatives that promote climate action, businesses can help create a regulatory environment that encourages sustainable practices. This chapter explores the role of businesses in climate advocacy and the importance of public-private partnerships in driving meaningful change. It also highlights the need for businesses to work together and share best practices to achieve collective climate goals.

Paragraph 4: The transition to a low-carbon economy presents both challenges and opportunities for businesses. While there may be short-term costs associated with adopting sustainable practices, there are also long-term benefits, such as increased resilience, improved reputation, and access to new markets. This chapter concludes by discussing the business case for climate action and the ways in which businesses can turn sustainability into a competitive advantage. It also emphasizes the importance of bold leadership and innovation in tackling climate change.

9

Chapter 9: The Influence of Corporate Culture on Business Success

Paragraph 1: Corporate culture refers to the values, beliefs, and behaviors that characterize an organization. A strong and positive corporate culture can significantly impact business success by fostering employee engagement, enhancing productivity, and promoting innovation. This chapter explores the elements of corporate culture and their influence on business performance. It examines the ways in which businesses can cultivate a culture that supports their strategic goals and values.

Paragraph 2: One key aspect of corporate culture is the alignment of organizational values with business practices. When employees feel that their values are aligned with those of the organization, they are more likely to be motivated and committed to their work. This chapter discusses the importance of value alignment and the role of leadership in shaping and reinforcing organizational values. It also highlights the need for businesses to communicate their values clearly and consistently to all stakeholders.

Paragraph 3: Another important dimension of corporate culture is the emphasis on collaboration and teamwork. A culture that promotes open communication, mutual respect, and shared goals can enhance teamwork and drive collective success. This chapter explores the ways in which businesses can foster a collaborative culture and the benefits of doing so. It also discusses the challenges of managing diverse teams and the strategies for building inclusive and cohesive work environments.

Paragraph 4: Corporate culture can also impact innovation and adaptability. A culture that encourages creativity, risk-taking, and continuous learning can drive innovation and help businesses respond to changing market conditions. This chapter examines the relationship between corporate culture and innovation, and the ways in which businesses can create an environment that supports experimentation and growth. It concludes by discussing the role of corporate culture in shaping the future of work and the importance of nurturing a culture that embraces change.

10

Chapter 10: The Role of Corporate Philanthropy in Society

Paragraph 1: Corporate philanthropy refers to the charitable activities and contributions made by businesses to support social and community causes. It is an important aspect of corporate social responsibility and reflects a business's commitment to giving back to society. This chapter explores the role of corporate philanthropy in addressing social issues and improving community well-being. It examines the various forms of corporate philanthropy and their impact on both businesses and society.

Paragraph 2: One common form of corporate philanthropy is financial donations to non-profit organizations and community projects. By providing financial support, businesses can help fund important initiatives and services that benefit society. This chapter discusses the importance of strategic philanthropy and the need for businesses to align their philanthropic efforts with their core values and goals. It also highlights the benefits of building long-term partnerships with non-profit organizations and community groups.

Paragraph 3: In addition to financial contributions, businesses can also engage in corporate volunteering and employee giving programs. By encouraging employees to volunteer their time and skills, businesses can create a positive social impact and foster a sense of purpose and engagement among their workforce. This chapter explores the benefits of corporate volunteering and the ways in which businesses can support and promote employee giving. It also discusses the importance of measuring the impact of philanthropic activities and communicating the results to stakeholders.

Paragraph 4: Corporate philanthropy can also enhance a business's reputation and strengthen its relationships with stakeholders. By demonstrating a commitment to social responsibility, businesses can build trust and goodwill with customers, employees, investors, and communities. This chapter concludes by discussing the strategic advantages of corporate philanthropy and the ways in which businesses can integrate philanthropy into their overall corporate strategy. It also emphasizes the need for businesses to be transparent and accountable in their philanthropic activities to ensure that their contributions are meaningful and effective.

11

Chapter 11: The Role of Business in Promoting Social Justice

Paragraph 1: Social justice refers to the fair and equitable distribution of resources, opportunities, and privileges within a society. Businesses have a significant role to play in promoting social justice by addressing inequalities and advocating for inclusive practices. This chapter explores the ways in which businesses can contribute to social justice and the importance of integrating social justice principles into their strategies. It examines the impact of business practices on marginalized communities and the ways in which businesses can promote fairness and equality.

Paragraph 2: One key area where businesses can promote social justice is in the workplace. By fostering diversity, equity, and inclusion (DEI), businesses can create a supportive and inclusive environment for all employees. This includes implementing policies that promote equal opportunities, addressing biases and discrimination, and providing support for underrepresented groups. This chapter discusses the benefits of DEI initiatives and the ways in which businesses can measure and track their progress in promoting social justice within their organizations.

Paragraph 3: Businesses can also promote social justice through their supply chains and procurement practices. By ensuring that their suppliers adhere to fair labor practices and ethical standards, businesses can help improve working conditions and support the rights of workers globally. This chapter explores the importance of responsible sourcing and the role of businesses in promoting social justice throughout their supply chains. It also discusses the challenges of monitoring and enforcing ethical practices and the ways in which businesses can collaborate with stakeholders to achieve their goals.

Paragraph 4: Beyond their operations, businesses can also advocate for social justice through their public engagement and advocacy efforts. By supporting policies and initiatives that promote equity and fairness, businesses can help drive systemic change and address the root causes of social injustice. This chapter concludes by discussing the role of businesses in social justice advocacy and the importance of partnering with non-profit organizations, government agencies, and community groups. It emphasizes the need for businesses to be vocal and proactive in their commitment to social justice and to use their influence to create positive change.

12

Chapter 12: The Future of Business: Integrating Profit and Purpose

Paragraph 1: As society evolves, so too must the role of business. The traditional focus on profit as the sole measure of success is giving way to a more holistic approach that integrates profit with purpose. This chapter explores the future of business and the importance of aligning business practices with broader societal goals. It examines the emerging trends and innovations that are shaping the future of business and the ways in which businesses can create value for both shareholders and society.

Paragraph 2: One key trend driving the future of business is the rise of stakeholder capitalism. This approach emphasizes the importance of considering the interests of all stakeholders, including employees, customers, suppliers, communities, and the environment. By prioritizing stakeholder value, businesses can create long-term, sustainable success and build stronger relationships with their stakeholders. This chapter discusses the principles of stakeholder capitalism and the strategies businesses can use to implement this approach.

Paragraph 3: Another important trend is the increasing emphasis on purpose-driven business models. Businesses that are driven by a clear and meaningful purpose are better positioned to attract and retain customers, employees, and investors. This chapter explores the ways in which businesses can define and communicate their purpose and align their operations with their mission and values. It also highlights the role of leadership in fostering a purpose-driven culture and the importance of authenticity and transparency.

Paragraph 4: The integration of profit and purpose requires businesses to rethink their strategies and embrace innovation. This includes adopting new technologies, business models, and partnerships that align with their purpose and create positive social and environmental impact. This chapter concludes by discussing the future of business and the ways in which businesses can navigate the challenges and opportunities of a rapidly changing world. It emphasizes the importance of agility, resilience, and a commitment to continuous learning and improvement.

13

Chapter 13: Navigating Ethical Dilemmas in Business

Paragraph 1: Ethical dilemmas are an inevitable aspect of business decision-making. These dilemmas arise when businesses face conflicting values, interests, or obligations, requiring them to make tough choices that can have significant consequences. This chapter explores the nature of ethical dilemmas in business and the frameworks that can guide ethical decision-making. It examines real-world examples of ethical dilemmas and the strategies that businesses can use to navigate these challenges.

Paragraph 2: One common ethical dilemma in business is the conflict between profit maximization and social responsibility. Businesses may face situations where pursuing profit could lead to negative social or environmental impacts. This chapter discusses the importance of balancing profit with ethical considerations and the role of corporate social responsibility in resolving ethical dilemmas. It also highlights the need for businesses to establish clear ethical guidelines and codes of conduct to guide their decision-making processes.

Paragraph 3: Transparency and accountability are crucial in addressing ethical dilemmas. Businesses must be open about their decision-making processes and the rationale behind their choices. This chapter explores the importance of stakeholder engagement and the need for businesses to communicate honestly with their stakeholders. It also discusses the role of leadership in setting the tone for ethical behavior and fostering a culture of integrity within the organization.

Paragraph 4: Ethical dilemmas can also arise in the context of global business operations. Different cultural norms, legal standards, and business practices can create complex ethical challenges for multinational corporations. This chapter examines the ways in which businesses can navigate these challenges and ensure that their operations are ethically sound across different regions. It concludes by discussing the importance of ethical leadership and the need for businesses to be proactive in identifying and addressing ethical issues.

14

Chapter 14: The Role of Innovation in Driving Business Growth

Paragraph 1: Innovation is a key driver of business growth and competitive advantage. It involves the development and implementation of new ideas, products, services, and processes that create value for customers and stakeholders. This chapter explores the role of innovation in business success and the strategies that businesses can use to foster a culture of innovation. It examines the different types of innovation, including incremental, disruptive, and open innovation, and their impact on business performance.

Paragraph 2: One important aspect of fostering innovation is creating an environment that encourages creativity and risk-taking. Businesses need to provide employees with the freedom and resources to experiment and explore new ideas. This chapter discusses the importance of fostering a culture of experimentation and the role of leadership in promoting innovation. It also highlights the benefits of collaboration and cross-functional teams in driving innovative solutions.

Paragraph 3: Technology plays a crucial role in enabling innovation. Advances in digital technologies, such as artificial intelligence, blockchain, and the Internet of Things, have created new opportunities for businesses to innovate and transform their operations. This chapter explores the ways in which businesses can leverage technology to drive innovation and the importance of staying ahead of technological trends. It also discusses the challenges of managing technological change and the need for businesses to invest in research and development.

Paragraph 4: The process of innovation is not without its challenges. Businesses may face obstacles such as resistance to change, resource constraints, and market uncertainties. This chapter examines the common barriers to innovation and the strategies that businesses can use to overcome them. It concludes by discussing the importance of continuous improvement and the need for businesses to be agile and adaptable in a rapidly changing world.

15

Chapter 15: Building Resilient Businesses for the Future

Paragraph 1: Resilience is the ability of businesses to withstand and adapt to challenges, disruptions, and uncertainties. In an increasingly volatile and unpredictable world, building resilience is essential for long-term success. This chapter explores the principles of business resilience and the strategies that businesses can use to enhance their resilience. It examines the various dimensions of resilience, including operational, financial, and organizational resilience.

Paragraph 2: One key aspect of building resilience is risk management. Businesses need to identify, assess, and mitigate risks that could impact their operations and performance. This chapter discusses the importance of risk management frameworks and the role of contingency planning in building resilience. It also highlights the need for businesses to be proactive in monitoring and responding to emerging risks and threats.

Paragraph 3: Financial resilience is another critical dimension of business resilience. Businesses need to maintain a strong financial position and ensure access to capital to weather economic downturns and other disruptions. This chapter explores the strategies for achieving financial resilience, such as diversification, cost management, and prudent financial planning. It also discusses the importance of building strong relationships with investors, lenders, and other financial stakeholders.

Paragraph 4: Organizational resilience is about building a resilient workforce and a supportive organizational culture. Businesses need to invest in employee well-being, development, and engagement to create a resilient and adaptable workforce. This chapter examines the ways in which businesses can foster a culture of resilience and the role of leadership in promoting resilience. It concludes by discussing the importance of continuous learning and the need for businesses to embrace change and innovation to thrive in a dynamic environment.

"The Policy of Profit: Rethinking Business Through the Lens of Politics and Society":

In "The Policy of Profit: Rethinking Business Through the Lens of Politics and Society," we embark on a comprehensive journey to uncover the intricate and evolving relationship between business, politics, and society. This thought-provoking book explores the complex interplay between corporate interests and political influence, shining a light on how businesses shape, and are shaped by, the regulatory and social landscape.

Chapter by chapter, we delve into critical topics such as the role of regulation in shaping business practices, the impact of corporate lobbying on public policy, and the importance of social responsibility and ethical business conduct. We examine how globalization and technological advancements are redefining business strategies and market dynamics, and we highlight the significance of corporate governance, culture, and philanthropy in driving sustainable success.

Through a blend of historical context, contemporary case studies, and forward-looking insights, "The Policy of Profit" challenges readers to rethink traditional notions of profit and success. It emphasizes the need for businesses to integrate profit with purpose, to adopt sustainable and socially responsible practices, and to advocate for social justice and climate action.

Ultimately, this book provides a roadmap for businesses to navigate the complexities of the modern world, where profit is no longer the sole metric of success. By reimagining their roles and responsibilities, businesses can

CHAPTER 15: BUILDING RESILIENT BUSINESSES FOR THE FUTURE

create lasting value for all stakeholders and contribute to a more just and equitable society.

www.ingramcontent.com/pod-product-compliance
Lightning Source LLC
LaVergne TN
LVHW020501080526
838202LV00057B/6092